T0146785

Operation Virtue

Bring Forth Your Hidden Treasures

LEONETTA JULES AND TYJANE' STEVENS

authorHOUSE®

AuthorHouse™
1663 Liberty Drive
Bloomington, IN 47403
www.authorhouse.com
Phone: 1 (800) 839-8640

Published by AuthorHouse 05/17/2018

ISBN: 978-1-5049-7878-1 (sc)
ISBN: 978-1-5049-7877-4 (e)

Contents

Acknowledgements

First giving thanks an honor to God, without his presence none of this would be possible. We would like to thank our parents, grandparents, loved ones, pastors, teachers and mentors who have helped to nurture and guide us on this journey. We have overcome many obstacles and if it weren't for the many avenues we have been given for release our outcome may have become very different.

Foreword

VIRTUE: a. Moral excellence and righteousness; goodness. 3. A particularly efficacious, good, or beneficial quality; advantage: Effective force or power:

Due to so many of the issues facing many women today, and with the knowledge that most of these issues stemmed from early childhood and teen years, we were led to create this daily devotional guide Operation Virtue. We wanted to instill Positive Knowledge, Courage, Love, and Virtue into the lives teen and tween girls and also women as young adults so that when they become adult women they can focus on their Purpose and not be Haunted by their Past.

The Inspirational Quotes were statuses that the Co-Author Naee Stevens put on Social Media. Upon our reading these statuses, our pastor at the time, Lenora Turner of Soul Winning Disciples Ministries in Hampton VA, made the suggestion that she turn her writings into a book to share with the world.

I pray that you will enjoy this book and that it will be useful in your daily walk with Christ as you embark on your own Road to Virtue. We know that Virtue is a Characteristic that is shaped and formed over time and therefore it is a mission for us to complete more so than it is anything else. I present to you......

Operation Virtue

Introduction

A story of Deliverance (True Story)
By Naee Le'Shaun Stevens on Thursday, July 5, 2012 at 11:14pm

Darkness. I could see nothing but I sensed I wasn't alone as I searched for some sign of life, I could hear whispers in my ear telling me death was at every corner, I was In a spiritual warfare as I fought endlessly at my own personal demons. I Ran. But I felt like I was on the path to nowhere, I was running to a finish line that didn't exist, And with every step I took, My breath seemed to Fade, Everything about me seemed to Disappear, And eventually I went into a State of Nothingness, I was alone, And There was No Sign of life that could Bring me back.

This was a dream that became a Reality; This was My life....Before I found Jesus.

I felt like a plane on auto-pilot, Drifting through life with no certain destination. Everything I did.....Was M E A N I N G L E S S. I was lost and could not be found, My friends; Oh how I longed to be like them, I wanted to feel what they felt, see what they saw, They seemed so happy. But In reality, all I wanted...Was Love.

I grew up the black sheep in the crowd. My family loved me to pieces, but I wanted more, I wanted to be accepted by people outside of my world, but they didn't. They teased me, they mocked me, and they cast me back into the darkness from which I came. The pain I felt from the tears I cried, Began to Spark a fire, in my heart. I became furious, bitter; I began taking my anger out on those who loved me the most. I began to lash out and hurt those who had only tried to help me. I was confused. Like I was being controlled by something unknown. I couldn't stand up to the people from whom I wanted acceptance. I should've been angry towards them, but I couldn't. The burning in my heart became a full-blown Rage, and I would be mad at everything and nothing at the same time. It was then I chose to seek A higher power, Something above me that could release the pain id been carrying for so long, It was then that I chose to seek God.

This is My Life, Now that I've found my purpose, now that I've Found God.

All I could do was cry; the love that I had been longing for was in Jesus. He has brought me so much joy that even when bad things happen, all I can do is smile and say "Thank you Jesus" My life has been altered. I am free, I am Living, I am Delivered :))

When I gave my heart to God, for the first time in my life...I felt Loved. I felt overwhelmed by the fact that someone could love me despite My flaws, In spite of everything I've done. That someone could love me even when I didn't even Acknowledge their existence. Someone could actually love me without trying to change anything about me, Loving me just as I am :') I kept trying to find that love from people, people who couldn't care less about where I made it or not. It brings tears to my eyes, knowing that When it comes to Jesus, There isn't A THING I have to do to prove myself to him, Nothing I could do to stop his love ♥

Communication

Psalms 19:14 says [14] Let the words of my mouth, and the meditation of my heart, be acceptable in thy sight, O Lord, my strength, and my redeemer.

The bible also teaches us that we speak life and death through the tongue, blessings and curses, and that it is the most unruly member of the body and to learn to tame it is considered a fruit of the spirit. It is easy to lash out from anger and hurt but it is hard to remain quiet even when you may be justified in speaking your mind. But the word says let this mind be in you that was also in Christ Jesus. The only thing that was on Jesus mind was doing his Father's will at any and all cost. So remember that the next time someone makes you upset or you feel like boasting on yourself for good works. Remember that Jesus endured all that he went through on the cross without saying a word, and that in life the only words he spoke were according to the will of his Father, and that Even God when he speaks to us, speaks in a still, small, voice.

Walk the Talk

Real people don't go around bragging about their position/status just like TRUE Christians don't walk around trying to prove to everybody that they're a Christian. If you really are what you say you are, you shouldn't have to broadcast it every day of your life. People can automatically tell by your Lifestyle. I've been told that people who always have something to say are liars. Your words should never contradict your actions.

Scripture: Matthew 23 1-7

23 Then Jesus said to the crowds and to his followers, ² "The teachers of the law and the Pharisees have the authority to tell you what the law of Moses says. ³ So you should obey and follow whatever they tell you, but their lives are not good examples for you to follow. They tell you to do things, but they themselves don't do them. ⁴ They make strict rules and try to force people to obey them, but they are unwilling to help those who struggle under the weight of their rules.

⁵ "They do good things so that other people will see them. They enlarge the little boxes[a] holding Scriptures that they wear, and they make their special prayer clothes very long. ⁶ Those Pharisees and teachers of the law love to have the most important seats at feasts and in the synagogues. ⁷ They love people to greet them with respect in the marketplaces, and they love to have people call them 'Teacher.'

Elaboration

There's a saying that says "Don't speak about it, Be about it", meaning practice what you preach. If you say you're about something, then everything about you should portray the image of what you say you are about. You don't see princesses wearing dirty jeans, messed up hair, and hanging around a bunch of nobodies, that want nothing and have nothing. No, they look and act like royalty and are only seen in the presence of royalty. Well if God is our father and we are his daughters and he is the King, then what does that make us....... Princesses. We have to learn to change our mindsets once we come into the Kingdome of God. We are now royalty and everything we do should be done in excellence. This doesn't mean we have to wear designer clothes and have all the latest shoes and accessories and all that. It just simply means take pride in yourself. If you have clothes with holes in them then throw them out and keep only the good ones. If you can't afford to get your hair done all the time then make sure your hair is clean and combed every day. Do an inventory of your company. If they want something out of life and are making moves to obtain those things, keep them and if not then drop them. Don't be mean because that's not Godly, just explain that you are taking you life in a different direction your trying to reach your goals and if they want to do the same then you would enjoy their company and if not you will have to love them from a distance but you have to look out for yourself and your future. It may be one of the hardest things you will have to do but the benefits in the long run are well worth it. You can't just say your different and still keep the same old ways. You have to Walk the Talk.

A True Friend

I've lost a lot of friends throughout my lifetime. But I asked God if it was in his will, let it be done, I'm thankful for the ones I still have, but I learned an important lesson over the years. At the end of the day, at some point your gonna have to learn to be your own friend, cause that's all your gonna have when you go :)

Scripture: John 15:15, 18-21

[15] I no longer call you servants, because a servant does not know what his master is doing. But I call you friends, because I have made known to you everything I heard from my Father.

[18] "If the world hates you, remember that it hated me first. [19] If you belonged to the world, it would love you as it loves its own. But I have chosen you out of the world, so you don't belong to it. That is why the world hates you. [20] Remember what I told you: A servant is not greater than his master. If people did wrong to me, they will do wrong to you, too. And if they obeyed my teaching, they will obey yours, too. [21] They will do all this to you on account of me, because they do not know the One who sent me

Elaboration

The definition of a friend is: **1.** A person whom one knows, likes, and trusts. One who supports another.

Now the first two characteristics (know and like) are criteria one would need to meet in order to be added to a "friend list" on a social media network. The last two however (Trust and support) require a lot more time and intimacy. In order to know if you can trust someone, they have to be tested. Not intentionally tested but over time there are some things you have been through together in which you have had to depend on that person either for support or for discretion. Meaning either they were there for you when no one else was or you have told, shown them or experienced something with them in confidence and it has not gone outside of the two of you.

Support on the other hand comes in many different forms. Some are easy such as attending an event when asked. Some are a little more intense, such as telling a person something they don't want to hear when you know that it may make them upset but they need to hear it because it is for their good. A "friend" is not always in agreement, not a yes man, but someone who can challenge your inner person and bring out the best in you all while respecting every aspect of your being and your relationship.

That is what God is to us. We bring out the best in him because he put his best in us. Jesus said we who believe in him are his friends because we are willing to suffer with him, so we will therefore reign with him. We take heed to his knowledge and wisdom and apply it to our lives because it will make us both better. And because we share his vision, which is building his father's kingdom, and work with him at any cost to make sure it comes to pass. If you have people around you that don't meet those criteria, then you need to redo your "friend" list and do some "deleting" from your life page. Only God knows how to be a true friend and any person who you are considering to fill that position in your life MUST have him also.

Hurt People Hurt People

There's one bible verse that always has me putting my feelings aside and remembering what's important, FORGIVE and you shall be FORGIVEN. God knows at times I want some people to hurt as much as they've hurt me. But the truth of the matter is, Hurt people only hurt other people.

All I can do is continue to pray that God continues to bless them and that they become prosperous. I'll continue to forgive my enemies, and those who have done me wrong. Not because it makes me the bigger person, But because I know I have hurt a lot of people in my life, including God, because of who I am today, I don't need to prove myself to anyone. I would want to be forgiven to.

Scripture: Matthew 6:14

[14] "For if you forgive men their trespasses, your heavenly Father will also forgive you. [15] But if you do not forgive men their trespasses, neither will your Father forgive your trespasses.

Elaboration

First of all let's take a look at the word **FORGIVE.** The word FOR means: Used to indicate the object, aim, or purpose of an action or activity. The word GIVE means: To place in the hands of; pass.

Now you may ask why we are going this route. Well let's take a look at what happens when we don't forgive one another. First un-forgiveness brings about hostility, Hostility brings about stress, stress brings about a myriad of health, emotional, physical, and mental issues. In fact the word disease, when broken down reads DIS EASE. Not to mention the spiritual repercussions associated with un-forgiveness. Un- forgiveness is the gateway by which all other sins enter the spirit. You can't even pray and be heard by God with ill feelings toward someone else in your heart. I'm not making that up its in Mark 11:25. And whenever you stand praying, if you have anything against anyone, forgive him and let it drop (leave it, let it go), in order that your Father Who is in heaven may also forgive you your [own] failings and shortcomings and let them drop.. If you allow this seed to take root in your heart it will allow other sins to attach themselves to it. Sins such as envy, strife, sewing discord(gossiping and plotting) and a list of others. Hurt people in turn hurt other people.

So now knowing what un-forgiveness does in your life now we can apply the definition from the beginning. The definition means to indicate the object, aim or purpose of an action or activity and place it in the hands of or pass.….it over to God.

Prayer

Prayer for good communication: Dear Lord, please help me to be conscious of the words I speak. Help me to be slow to speak and quick to hear. Help me to only say uplifting and encouraging words that will build and never tear down. Help me to protect my heart and only allow inspiring words to leave my mouth. In Jesus' Name. Amen.

Goal

_____

_____

_____

_____

Steps I Need to Take to Reach This Goal

_____

_____

_____

_____

_____

_____

Faith

Hebrews 11:1 says 11 Now faith is confidence in what we hope for and assurance about what we do not see.

God showed me an acronym for Now Faith.

Need **O**f **W**orks **F**or **A**ll **I**ntended **T**o **H**appen. This means that in order for faith to be activated it needs to be followed by some action. The bible says Faith without Works is dead. Look at it this way, If you are nervous about passing a test, and you pray for God to help you pass it, well you have to first study and then actually go and take the test with the faith that God will be with you. What God does is bring back to your remembrance the things you studied, therefore helping you pass the test. You can't just do nothing and expect the answers to fall from the sky and you automatically pass the test, that's not faith that's wishful thinking. Sometimes your works will require you making the first step and allowing God to make the rest, while some works will require you being patient and waiting on God to do what you're having faith for him to do. Waiting doesn't mean twiddling your thumbs, it means going on with your life asking God to lead and guide you through prayer for the path you should be on so that you can be in position to receive his promise of that which you are having faith for him to come through on.

Mission Possible

The enemy is on a mission to steal, kill, and destroy every spiritual part of me, and make me a non-believer. But I've come too far to give up now;

this is just a test, Im walking by faith and not by sight. And even if it takes everything I have left, im NOT going out without a fight. I'm about to give my all to God, he's my focus from now on. Cutting off EVERYTHING that's gonna tear me from my walk with god, I want to feel how I felt when I first fell in love with JESUS ♥.

Scripture: John 10: 7-10

[7] Then Jesus said to them again, "Most assuredly, I say to you, I am the door of the sheep. [8] All who *ever* came before Me[a] are thieves and robbers, but the sheep did not hear them. [9] I am the door. If anyone enters by Me, he will be saved, and will go in and out and find pasture. [10] The thief does not come except to steal, and to kill, and to destroy. I have come that they may have life, and that they may have *it* more abundantly.

Elaboration

Most of the time we can tell when someone is out to get us. We can feel the bad vibes or see the change in relationship, or circumstances around us. However the enemy, also known as "Satan" or "The Devil", is a lot more subtle than that. In the Bible it talks about how the serpent came to deceive eve about eating of the tree of good and evil. He told her that God only told her not to eat of it because he didn't want her to be like him and know good and evil things like the Gods. What she didn't realize was that she already knew good and evil. Good was being obedient to what she was told and Evil was being disobedient. The enemy knows what we are weak in and he deceives us using those things. If we long for attention he will send people into our lives that will pay us compliments, and want to be around us all the time and really make us feel wanted. Then we get a false sense of loyalty and love from these people and when they begin to do things that go against our character, we tend to go along with them because we **THINK** they are our friends and have our best interest at heart. All along it was an elaborate scheme by the enemy to keep us from doing what we are purposed to do, whatever it is. Then when we feel bad about the place we are in because of the Mistakes we've made, he burdens us with so much guilt we cannot even get back to the place we were in before not to mention elevating to a higher place.

Just remember we have to ask God daily for guidance and to help us Discern (separate) what is good for us and what is not. Just know there is nothing we can do that will make God stop loving us and he will always except us back into his arms as long as we are willing to ask forgiveness and start again. It is a mission, but it's a mission that can be completed. We call it Mission Possible.

Prayer

Prayer of Faith: Dear Lord, I thank you the gift of faith. As I grow my mustard seed faith into great faith, I know many great things will happen on my behalf. Please help me to stay focused on your word rather than what my human eyes can see, for I know your word has never changed and it pleases you when I show faith. In Jesus' Name. Amen.

Goal

_____

_____

_____

_____

Steps I Need to Take to Reach This Goal

_____

_____

_____

_____

_____

_____

_____

Patience

Isaiah 40:31 says [31] But they that wait upon the LORD shall renew their strength; they shall mount up with wings as eagles; they shall run, and not be weary; and they shall walk, and not faint.

Patience is a Virtue they say. Meaning that it is considered a fruit of God's spirit for one to have Patience. But be careful when praying for patience because the only way to get patience it for God to make you wait for something you really want.

My brother is in the army, and he said that when he was in basic training the drill sergeants made them sit in the hot sun waiting for hours some times for their next activity and if they were caught murmuring or complaining they were penalized. Sometimes they would move on quickly and sometimes it would take forever, but by the time it was all over they learned to be patient and just wait peacefully because eventually it was gonna come. They just had to be ready and in position when the time came. We are no different, we are soldiers in the army of the Lord and the same rules apply. Soldiers are an example to civilians of how to be disciplined and moral and just. Christians are supposed to be an example to the world of the same.

A Virtuous Woman

I told my mommy that guy's who love to embrace their spirituality are my weakness, and that it's all I ever wanted in a person. But I asked why is it that when I meet one, I can never have them, but can come across all the wrong ones so easily. She told me that the bible says a man who findeth a WIFE findeth a good thing, and good things come to those who wait. I can't be found if I'm too busy looking. She made my day ♥

Scripture: Proverbs 31: 10-31

The Good Wife

¹⁰ It is hard to find a good wife,
because she is worth more than rubies.
¹¹ Her husband trusts her completely.
With her, he has everything he needs.
¹² She does him good and not harm
for as long as she lives.
¹³ She looks for wool and flax
and likes to work with her hands.
¹⁴ She is like a trader's ship,
bringing food from far away.
¹⁵ She gets up while it is still dark
and prepares food for her family
and feeds her servant girls.
¹⁶ She inspects a field and buys it.
With money she earned, she plants a vineyard.
¹⁷ She does her work with energy,
and her arms are strong.
¹⁸ She knows that what she makes is good.
Her lamp burns late into the night.
¹⁹ She makes thread with her hands
and weaves her own cloth.
²⁰ She welcomes the poor
and helps the needy.
²¹ She does not worry about her family when it snows,
because they all have fine clothes to keep them warm.
²² She makes coverings for herself;
her clothes are made of linen and other expensive material.

[23] Her husband is known at the city meetings,
where he makes decisions as one of the leaders of the land.
[24] She makes linen clothes and sells them
and provides belts to the merchants.
[25] She is strong and is respected by the people.
She looks forward to the future with joy.
[26] She speaks wise words
and teaches others to be kind.
[27] She watches over her family

and never wastes her time.
[28] Her children speak well of her.
Her husband also praises her,
[29] saying, "There are many fine women,
but you are better than all of them."
[30] Charm can fool you, and beauty can trick you,
but a woman who respects the LORD should be praised.
[31] Give her the reward she has earned;
she should be praised in public for what she has done.

Elaboration

In Genesis chapter 2 and verses 20-25, It tells us why God created a mate for Adam in the first place. There was a need. Adam had been given this great responsibility and everything that God created had a mate to help it in its purpose and to multiply the species. However He could see that Adam was lonely and needed help with this Great responsibility he was given. He didn't give him a mate because Adam just wanted one because Adam didn't even know what he wanted yet. He gave it to him because there was a specific need that coincided particularly with God's plan.

Secondly God put him in a deep sleep as he performed this work of art, so Adam was not looking for his mate because he had no idea what was happening behind the scenes. Eve was not presented to him until God was finished. Finished doing what exactly you may ask. Well that's the good part. Being that Adam and Eve were the first, they didn't know what trials and work would face them in the future so they didn't even know what to expect of each other. But God knew. He had already given Adam his instructions, now Eve needed hers.

The passage above is God's Idea of a virtuous woman. Meaning the perfect woman, the total package. God had to create more than someone that looked just like Adam. Every detail had a purpose. Everything about her was a compliment to what Adam needed. For instance, even though Adam and eve were never babies, God knew how the babies were going to have to eat so he gave Eve breasts and filled them with glands that would produce milk and have all the nutrients that a baby would need to grow up big and strong. God was telling and teaching Eve everything she needed to know in order to be the perfect help mate for Adam who had this great responsibility of keeping and managing everything that God created.

Long story short, if you are wondering why you are still single, or always running into the wrong guys, then you need to step back and inventory yourself. Use the "Virtuous Woman" as your guide. God is molding and shaping you to be the perfect mate for someone. If you keep running into the wrong ones it's because you are on the wrong path. God created a work of art in Eve and taught and molded her into everything that Adam would need and then he presented her to him when he was done. She didn't go looking for him, he didn't go looking for her. God put them together when his work in the both of them was completed. So stop looking for your mate and let God finish creating the work of art that is you and allow him to present you to your mate who he has fashioned just for you and you for him. Concentrate on being a Virtuous Woman who's worth is priceless, don't sell yourself short of the perfection God has created.

You deserve a Real Love

Just got through talking to My Best friend, and it made me realize things about myself that I didn't want to face before. It's a terrible thing for anyone to be in a relationship w/ a sorry excuse for a significant other just because their infatuated with the person they want them to be and blinded about who they really are. It's everything BUT love, and it can trap you in your own fantasy world outside from reality. Don't ever lower your standards or settle for less, cause if they don't have it now they never will. It's when YOU decide you deserve better, that you become available to better ♥

Scripture: 1 Corinthians 13:4-10

[4] Love suffers long *and* is kind; love does not envy; love does not parade itself, is not puffed up; [5] does not behave rudely, does not seek its own, is not provoked, thinks no evil; [6] does not rejoice in iniquity, but rejoices in the truth; [7] bears all things, believes all things, hopes all things, endures all things.[8] Love never fails. But whether *there are* prophecies, they will fail; whether *there are* tongues, they will cease; whether *there is* knowledge, it will vanish away. [9] For we know in part and we prophesy in part. [10] But when that which is perfect has come, then that which is in part will be done away.

Elaboration

L. O. V. E. That s a word that seems to get a lot of people in trouble. Mostly because they do not know the true meaning of it. People seem to throw the word around so loosely. They use it to in order to gain things that they desire. They use it because they want to make someone else feel good. They use it to gain alliances. They even get it mixed up with lust and infatuation. In fact **LOVE** is not an emotion at all. It is indeed a verb. That's right, it is an action. Love is what remains when emotions wear off. 1 Corinthians 13:4-10 describes to us perfectly just exactly what love is and what it does.

John 15:9-14 says [9] "As the Father has loved me, so have I loved you. Now remain in my love. [10] If you keep my commands, you will remain in my love, just as I have kept my Father's commands and remain in his love. [11] I have told you this so that my joy may be in you and that your joy may be complete. [12] My command is this: Love each other as I have loved you. [13] Greater love has no one than this: to lay down one's life for one's friends. [14] You are my friends if you do what I command.

This is the perfect picture that God has painted for us through his son Jesus Christ. You see in order to know real true love, we have to first get to know the person who is love. **GOD IS LOVE** plain and simple. So before you buy into someone telling you that they love you, or before you decide to let those words so loosely leak from your own lips, measure up. Use the scriptures of 1 Corinthians 13 and John 15 as a guide and see if you display those characteristics or it the person you are hearing it from does. Furthermore see if they have a real true relationship with God the father. He paid the ultimate price for you and you deserve a real love.

A Man That Findeth A Wife

A woman's mind, body, heart and soul should be so concealed in God, that a man would have to seek HIM to find HER :) that's just how it works. God should always be the foundation to any relationship, period. Without him, it would only be temporary, and it surely will die.

Scripture: Proverbs 18:22

[22] When a man finds a wife, he finds something good.
It shows that the LORD is pleased with him.

Elaboration

Now it's time to put the whole thing into perspective. The reason for the virtuous Woman. See the reason that you are learning how to be Virtuous now is so that later you can be that "Good Thing" that the bible speaks about a man finding. You see, all the things you are going through now are Gods way of pruning and grooming you for your mate who he has fashioned just for You. Meaning everything you have will be exactly what h needs. Some things were with you at birth (and it has nothing to do with body parts, I mean the gifts and traits and personality God gave you) and some things came about through experience. In the end they all had a purpose.

As far as your future soul mate, well God is working on him as well. When a prince sees a princess and wants to court her, he does not approach her and ask her for a date. He has to go humbly before the King and ask permission to court her. The King, being that he has been grooming and raising his daughter a certain way, will examine the young prince to see if he is the right fit for his princess based on what he has put in her. If he sees fit he will grant permission if not then she will just have to wait until he sees a prince that will suite her. Well that is what God is to us. He is the Most High King and we are his daughters, therefore making us princesses. Any man who wants to inherit our heart must go humbly before the King to get his permission. Don't just accept any body into your life and your heart. Just sit back and wait for the King to grant permission to the right one. The one that has been waiting for his other half and respects you enough to get to know your father and find out what his wishes are for you. You are that good thing so don't settle for anyone that would consider you any less than that. Only God knows who will appreciate and cherish you for what you have. Wait on HIM, Oh Virtuous Woman, PRINCESS DAUGHTER OF ZION. Be Blessed!!!

Be the example, True love waits

A lot of people always ask me why I'm waiting as long as I am to give myself away. They ask me "what's taking you so long' or "what you got to lose". I made a PROMISE to god that I would do his will and not my own. I'm too good of a person to be somebody's play toy. Sex is 95% of a relationship these days, I feel like I deserve better than what I've gotten. I could care less at this point whose against it. I know that in the end I'll be greatly rewarded. I AM worth it :)

Scripture: 1 Timothy 4:12

[12] Let no one despise your youth, but be an example to the believers in word, in conduct, in love, in spirit,[b] in faith, in purity.

Elaboration

It seems the term worth the wait has almost become cliché. Like everyone is saying it and it has become a popular trend. But what happens after the purity ball, and the virtue ceremonies, and the point when our friends start to slip and everyone around you has a boyfriend as has forgotten about their vows. Well this is what sets you apart from everyone else. It has even gotten to a point where even the guys don't believe it when they hear it. I have heard so many times when a girl tells a guy she is a virgin and waiting until marriage, he will say "so and so said that and now she has a baby" or "girls always say that and then the next thing you know they have gone wild". So my next question is what are you doing it for. Fads and trends are just that. There here today and gone tomorrow, so if that is why you are doing it then it will fade. We have to make sure that we do not take vows, and oaths, and make promises just because it is the thing to do. God takes these things seriously and we are held accountable for our word. We will have to answer to it one day. The bible says only what you do for Christ will last. So make sure that if you really want it to last you are doing it solely to please him because you recognize that your body is a temple and you want to be pure and untainted for God to use you the way he wishes too. Just make believe that he is on the inside and you wouldn't want to do anything with him in there that would make him uncomfortable.

This does not mean that if you have already "gone there" that you are not fit for service. Nothing could be farther from the truth. We call them "Re-Virgins". You just make the commitment that from this day forward you will abstain from sex and the bible says God places it as far as the east is from the west and he remembers it no more. It's like it never even happened in his eyes and all that he sees is now. It's not just a catch phrase, true love really does wait and is someone really does love you they will respect your wishes and respect you for standing for what you will believe in, and in fact it should make them love you more, it makes God love you more. Be the Example.

Prayer

Prayer for patience: Dear Lord, in the name of Jesus. I pray that I'm careful for nothing; never anxious, but in everything I do, I do by prayer and supplication with thanksgiving. Amen

Goal

_____

_____

_____

_____

Steps I Need to Take to Reach This Goal

_____

_____

_____

_____

_____

_____

_____

_____

Wisdom

Proverbs 2

My son, if you accept my words **and store up my commands within you,**
²turning your ear to wisdom
and applying your heart to understanding—
³indeed, if you call out for insight
and cry aloud for understanding,
⁴and if you look for it as for silver
and search for it as for hidden treasure,
⁵then you will understand the fear of the Lord
and find the knowledge of God.
⁶For the Lord **gives wisdom;**
from his mouth come knowledge and understanding

This word is telling us that wisdom is like a hidden treasure. It is hard to obtain but once you have it you are set. Wisdom is what helps you to make good decisions and keeps you out of trouble. Wisdom also helps you to teach others to do the same. Wisdom comes with experience. When you were little girls and someone told you not to do something and you did it anyway then you suffered the consequences, then you gained wisdom of what could happen when you did it and hopefully you learned not to do it again. Wisdom is gained from experience, either good or bad, weather you dodged a bullet or took one, you gained wisdom from the incident. God wants to give us wisdom in the same way, by experiencing Him.

Learning to Leave it to the Master

"God grant me the serenity to accept the things I cannot change, the courage to change the things I can, and the wisdom to know the difference." A lot of times I find myself trying to handle situations only God can deal with. Including choosing my friends, and my path in life, and a lot of times I fail. I'm growing wiser and stronger every day. I'll continue to love on God's people as long as God is my love.

Scripture: Psalm 143: 10

Teach me to do Your will, for You are my God; let Your good Spirit lead me into a level country and into the land of uprightness.

Elaboration

Often times we try to do a job that we have absolutely no qualifications for. It is a job that we have all tried to complete simultaneously and over time the evidence of our epic failure has resulted. It has resulted in prayer being taken out of schools, the lack of family interaction, the extinction of the nuclear family, overcrowding of jails, the increase of human trafficking and child pornography, the rise in crime of all types, the spiraling downfall of the importance of the church in the community, the list goes on and on. The Job I'm speaking of is the job of running our lives. In the day of our ancestors, even just as recent as the early 1900's, next to nothing was done without first consulting God. They prayed as a family before beginning the day and also before the completion of the day. They also ate as a family and said grace before dinner to give thanks to God for BEING THEIR PROVIDER. They knew that even though the effort was done by the family as a whole, it was by nothing but the direction of the Holy spirit that made it possible. And that whatever they didn't have at the time God would make it so that it would not be a miss that was detrimental to the family unit.

In this day and time everyone is out for self. We eat when we want to, sleep when we want to, and go and come as we please. There is no structure much less any time set aside for consulting God on anything. Though it is true that the traditions of old were more about religious practices than relationship with God, At least everyone was on one accord. We need to combine the two in a healthy manner so that the two will work together as one. Relationship and religion. We have to know that we must leave everything to the master because only he knows our fate. He is the author and finisher of it. We must learn to act only according to the Direction of the Holy spirit. We need to know that the only way to gain any control is to lose it first. Leave it to the Master.

Elevation is what it's called

It's when you come from even the worst of situations with a smile on your face that makes you capable of appreciating them when they're over. Sometimes the bad things that happen in your life aren't always meant to hurt you, although they do. It just means That god is getting ready to take you to a place where the things you thought you wanted cannot compare to what god has in store for you. The people you thought you needed do not fit into the vision god has for your life. Elevation is what It's called. After all, they say Light and Darkness can not dwell in the same place :)

Scripture: 2 Corinthians 6:14

[14] Be ye not unequally yoked together with unbelievers: for what fellowship hath righteousness with unrighteousness? and what communion hath light with darkness?

Elaboration

Once we accept God as our personal Lord and Savior, things immediately begin to change. It may even seem like things are getting worse. Like we are being attacked for no reason. That is true but not the way you may think.

When you enter a dark room and turn on the light the darkness goes away. Now everything that you could not see is now exposed. Well that is exactly what happens once we allow God to come inside of us. He is the light and once we begin to go back into those dark places we were in before we let him in, he begins to expose things for what they really are. Things and people who are in the dark and don't want to come out will begin to get angry and that is where the attacks come from. But don't worry, once you have Him on your side you do not have to battle anymore, he does it all for you. All you have to do is sit back and let him do all the work. Trust him and he will make you come out on top. He will begin to shave away all the people and things from around you that are not a part of his will for you. This process can be a little painful but it is more than worth it. It's just like being 500 pounds and trying to get through a door way. All those excess pounds have to be shaved off before you can fit through the door, but it's a process. Once the dead weight is gone you can go through the door into a new chapter.

No one ever turns on darkness, you can only turn on the light. The light controls the conditions of the room. Once the light comes on the darkness has to go away, they cannot be in the same place at the same time. Just remember this is what God does for us once we allow him in. And you know that once the light is on everything is so much brighter is better. You can see things in a way you've never seen before. Allow God to shave those pounds and come through the door into your destiny. Elevation is what it's called.

Prayer

Prayer for wisdom: Dear Lord, I pray today that I'm overtaken with wisdom. I pray that I stand on your word as I make my daily decisions on today. Guide my thoughts and words and help me to be conscious of what I stand for as a child of God. I pray that your words which I have in my heart be made available when I am face any difficult situation, so that you may get the glory from my life. In Jesus' name.

Goal

_____

_____

_____

_____

Steps I Need to Take to Reach This Goal

_____

_____

_____

_____

_____

_____

_____

Lifestyle

1 Peter 2:11 says Beloved, I urge you as sojourners and exiles to abstain from the passions of the flesh, which wage war against your soul.

God loves us so much that he warns us all throughout the bible that our flesh is evil, filthy and vile and that we should avoid trying to please it because it will only lead us to a life of heartache. He knows however that the majority of us won't listen, that's where his Grace and Mercy comes in. The scripture above tells us that pleasing the flesh wages war against our soul. This is because the bible tells us that the spirit and the flesh are against each other and they are designed this way so that we would not do what we want if we live by the Spirit of God, because when the spirit is strong it will bring the flesh into submission. Meaning it will do what God intends for it to do and not what it wants to do. The only way to be able to have this type of power is to have a Godly Lifestyle.

If you don't stand for something
You'll fall for anything

Never downplay your morals and standards to enhance someone's happiness. if someone cares about you and respects you then compromising your beliefs shouldn't even have to be questioned. They will love you for who you are, the person you have no choice but to be, than to tolerate you for pretending.

Scripture: Living Sacrifices to God

12 I beseech you therefore, brethren, by the mercies of God, that you present your bodies a living sacrifice, holy, acceptable to God, *which is* your reasonable service. [2] And do not be conformed to this world, but be transformed by the renewing of your mind, that you may prove what *is* that good and acceptable and perfect will of God.

Elaboration

Ladies, ladies, ladies. Its far past time that we stop allowing ourselves to be tolerated by people and start to be celebrated. You are a work of art, not an afterthought. Don't you know that even though people may not agree with the things that you stand for, they will respect you for standing for them un-shakeably. Meaning that you will not be shaken down from your beliefs in order to gain popularity, money, fame or any other thing that the world has to offer. Respect will get you a lot farther than popularity any day. While it may not look like it in the beginning it pays off in the end. We are bought with a price because God gave his only soon as the ultimate sacrifice so that we would not have to endure any other hardships alone as long as we conform to His ways. If you don't stand for God then you will fall for anything that the enemy throws your direction because you will have no standards to keep you grounded. Our bodies are to be used strictly as living sacrifices to God. We are not to use them for our own agendas because we are here to please him and bring him Glory. Anything else is only going to bring us shame and heartache. Stand for God or fall by the wayside.

Lord Make me Over

Starting Monday, we're going on a fast for a whole week. No hanging out, no texts or calls, no internet, no fast food. The time I use to occupy myself with these things will be given to God. He deserves it, its time I take the time out to thank god for all he's done for me, to show him that I can yield to the ways of Jesus and not to my own flesh. That I CAN put him first. Once I come off this fast, things are gonna be a lot different, I'm determined ♥ Monday 10/22/2012

Scripture: Psalms 51:10-13

[10] Create in me a clean heart, O God,
And renew a steadfast spirit within me.
[11] Do not cast me away from Your presence,
And do not take Your Holy Spirit from me.

[12] Restore to me the joy of Your salvation,
And uphold me *by Your* generous Spirit.
[13] *Then* I will teach transgressors Your ways,
And sinners shall be converted to You.

Elaboration

There comes a point in time, a point in life when we have to own up to the fact that the same old stuff just ain't gonna get it anymore. We all at some point have to know that we can't keep doing the same old things and expect to get different results. Just like we cannot be adults and try to wear the same clothes we did when we were infants, we can't expect to call ourselves grown and still think immaturely. With that being said, now is the time for a makeover. We often have no problem going to the beauty salon and getting a physical makeover, or going shopping to give our wardrobe a makeover, but we seldom take seriously the need to make over our spiritual lives. Without the refreshing and revival and renewal of the spirit we are just zombies anyway...... the walking dead

It may seem like it is easy to just give up certain behaviors and habits. We often say "I can stop doing that any time I want" Well, that's only half true. If you want to change you can make a conscious decision to do so but you cannot in your own strength overpower your flesh without your spirit and will being stronger than your flesh. Well the only way to conquer your flesh is by fasting. Fasting is the practice of denying your body something it enjoys and replacing it with something that will strengthen your spirit. For instance, if you like to watch a certain TV show, you would replace that 30 minutes of watching the show with reading the bible or praying or both. In doing this we show God that we are serious about seeking him for change. It shows him that we want to hear from him so badly that we are willing to give up our will to receive his will. "Not our will, but thy will be done". When this is done with sincerity, he will open up the windows of heaven and shower down the desires of your heart, because now he knows that your heart matches his, and that is his will. Lord Make Me Over!!!!!

Don't Judge Me

Mistakes are made every day so that we can use the knowledge we learned from them to prevent them in the future ♥ I'm done dealing with people who can't accept me for me, I'm done trying to impress people who, at the end of the day are not going to be there, I'm done sitting around waiting for things to happen, Instead of taking the chance to make them happen myself, I'm done wishing.

Scripture: Proverbs 24:16

[16] For a righteous *man* may fall seven times
And rise again,
But the wicked shall fall by calamity.

Elaboration

The definition for mistake is: **1.** An error or fault resulting from defective judgment, deficient knowledge, or carelessness.

Sometimes in life we exercise the practice of "mistaking". Weather its mistaking the type of people we have surrounded ourselves with, or mistaking the outcome of something and wasting time because we are in expectation of one thing happening and it goes a totally different way.

The good thing about mistakes is that they have purpose. If we never did anything wrong, how would we ever know what the right thing is. In addition to that, we can help someone else along the way because now we have gained "experience". Have you ever heard the phrase "experience is the best teacher".? Well it is the truth. Someone can tell you something a thousand times but until you get a personal experience with it, sometimes it just doesn't hit home and snap into place.

Some things you don't want to gain experience from though. You don't want to experience being paralyzed if you don't have to, so why not listen to someone when they tell you not to walk out in front of a bus. That is what the Holy spirit does, he tells us not to walk in front of the bus. But when we don't listen he will be there to pick up the pieces and help put us back together. So if you've made mistakes don't beat yourself up. Ask God for forgiveness for not listening to him. Ask him to fine tune your ears so you can hear him better, and start over again. The important thing is that you learn from your mistakes and not repeat them. If anyone tries to remind you of your past tell them "Don't Judge Me". Only God can do that and he judged you and found you fit for redemption.

Prayer

Prayer for a Godly lifestyle: Dear Lord, I thank you for your Word which teaches me that I am made in the image of you, I know am the salt of the earth and I am the light of the world. Help me to continue to be that greater light in such a dark world, not allowing the tricks of the enemy to deter me from living a Christ-like lifestyle. In Jesus' name.

Goal

_____

_____

_____

_____

Steps I Need to Take to Reach This Goal

_____

_____

_____

_____

_____

_____

Good Thoughts

Proverbs 17:22 A joyful heart is good medicine, but a crushed spirit dries up the bones.

It is a commonly known fact now that stress can and will **Kill** you. In fact the word disease when broken down means DIS EASE. The bible teaches us that we should focus on the things of God in heaven and let earthly things take care of themselves. When we worry and stress, or even when we consume our minds with things that are ungodly, we open ourselves up to all types of idle thoughts. Idle meaning that they are not productive, they won't get us anywhere in our lives. The word says such as a man thinketh so is he. So if you are constantly worried then you become worrisome. If you let problems burden you then you become problematic, if you set your mind on things and people you can't forgive then you become unforgiveable. If you think instead of the things you do have and things that are going well then God will bless you with more because you will have the attitude to go and get it. Nothing can stop you.

The Eye of the Beholder

This is to every girl who has fallen subject to SOCIETY'S version of beautiful. All the makeup, clothes, and jewelry will surely fade. True beauty is in the eye of the beholder. "Beauty lies Not within a Girl's Appearance, But within the essence of Her Spirit, her ability to Be strong Because she can see her weaknesses, To be fearless because she has been afraid, to love because she has hated, To be wise because she has been foolish, and to Smile....Because she has Felt sadness"

Scripture: Genesis 1:26-28

²⁶ Then God said, "Let us make human beings in our image and likeness. And let them rule over the fish in the sea and the birds in the sky, over the tame animals, over all the earth, and over all the small crawling animals on the earth."

²⁷ So God created human beings in his image. In the image of God he created them. He created them male and female. ²⁸ God blessed them and said, "Have many children and grow in number. Fill the earth and be its master. Rule over the fish in the sea and over the birds in the sky and over every living thing that moves on the earth."

Elaboration

What we have to realize is that beauty starts within. Have you ever seen a really attractive person and as soon as they open their mouth to speak, suddenly they don't look so good anymore. On the flip side, sometimes you meet someone who may not be all that attractive but there's just something about their smile or their eyes or the way they speak that is captivating. Well what you are experiencing is the spirit of God. The bible tells us that Jesus was not "easy to look upon" and that was for a reason. God wanted people to pay attention to what he had to say and not be popular because of the way he looked. God made us in his image meaning it is his spirit that is attractive and draws people, when they're being drawn to the right thing. This doesn't mean all pretty people are bad and all unattractive people are good. It just simply means that beauty starts within and radiates outward. When you feel good about yourself and you have Gods heart and you know that HE loves you unconditionally, then that light begins to show up on the outside and shows up a BEAUTY. Remember beauty is in the eye of the beholder and the Joy, Peace and Love of the Almighty God is a wonder to Behold.

Nobody but ME

I've been a subject to low self-esteem for as long as I can remember, and it held me back from being the person that Nobody else can be, Me. But I'm here to declare that the devil is a liar. For he who is in me is greater than he who is in the world. The god I serve can have you walking around with so much confidence,....that people mistake it for ARROGANCE:

Scripture: 1 John 4: 4-6

[4] You are of God, little children, and have overcome them, because He who is in you is greater than he who is in the world. [5] They are of the world. Therefore they speak *as* of the world, and the world hears them. [6] We are of God. He who knows God hears us; he who is not of God does not hear us. By this we know the spirit of truth and the spirit of error.

Elaboration

The definition of Self Esteem is: a confidence and satisfaction in oneself: SELF-RESPECT.

Notice that nowhere in the definition does it mention someone else. The definition has to do with the way you esteem yourself. Sadly however, we allow the way other people see us determine the way we see ourselves. This is an all too common practice. We are made in the image of God. Everything that is good and perfect about God, he used to create us. Male and Female. He is kind, patient loving, nurturing, strong, bold, hard working, a provider, determined, intelligent, authoritative, beautiful, joyful, etc. If there are any traits that you don't find in yourself, guess where you can get it from. That's right. It's already in you. You just have to pray and ask God to help you tap into it. Just remember it may not come they way you may think. For instance, if you require more patience then you will be required to wait for some things. If you need boldness then you will be put into situations where you will need to be bold. If you need to more humility than you will be put in situations that will humiliate you. That's just how it works. Just know that it is all to better your and help you to have those things that will make you complete. Once you know that God has created you perfectly in his image, and that whatever you don't display upfront, is still in you waiting to be tapped into, then you can begin to feel better about yourself. Then you will know that the people that don't appreciate you for who you are do so because they do not yet know who they are. Just stand your ground, believe in yourself, know that greater is he that is in you than he that is in the world, and no one can be the greatest thing God ever created accept you because it is **YOU**.

Prayer

Prayer for your thoughts: Lord, I pray today that you help me to control my thoughts. Help me to not think any evil towards anyone or anything, yet help me to think on things which are true, honest, just, pure, lovely, of a good report, of virtue and of praise. In the might name of Jesus.

Goal

_____

_____

_____

_____

Steps I Need to Take to Reach This Goal

_____

_____

_____

_____

_____

_____

_____

Prayers

Philippians 4:6 Do not be anxious about anything, but in everything by prayer and supplication with thanksgiving let your requests be made known to God.

This word is telling us to pray about everything and worry about nothing. Since God is the author and finisher of our fate and he sees and knows all, why not leave everything in his hands. If you don't know how or what to pray, the following section can help you get started until you are comfortable enough to speak to god yourself from your own heart.

Examples of Prayer

<u>Salvation</u> • <u>A Christian Struggling with Sin</u> • <u>Wisdom & Direction</u> • <u>Physical Healing</u> • <u>Comfort</u> • <u>Faith & Trust</u> • <u>Protection</u>

Salvation:

[8] If we claim to be without sin, we deceive ourselves and the truth is not in us.[9] If we confess our sins, he is faithful and just and will forgive us our sins and purify us from all unrighteousness. (1 John 1:8-9)

[9] That if you confess with your mouth, "Jesus is Lord," and believe in your heart that God raised him from the dead, you will be saved.[10] For it is with

your heart that you believe and are justified, and it is with your mouth that you confess and are saved. (Romans 10:9-10)

Suggested Prayer

Dear God,

I confess that I am a sinner and I have not lived my life for you. I ask forgiveness for my sins. I believe Jesus is your only Son and that He died on the cross for my sins and you raised Him from the dead. I receive Jesus Christ now as my Lord and Savior. I turn my life over to Him and ask you to change me from the inside out. Thank you for your salvation to me. In the name of Jesus, I pray. Amen.

A Christian struggling with sin:

[1]Have mercy on me, O God, according to your unfailing love; according to your great compassion blot out my transgressions.[2]Wash away all my iniquity and cleanse me from my sin.[3]For I know my transgressions, and my sin is always before me.[4]Against you, you only, have I sinned and done what is evil in your sight, so that you are proved right when you speak and justified when you judge.

[10]Create in me a pure heart, O God, and renew a steadfast spirit within me.[11]Do not cast me from your presence or take your Holy Spirit from me.[12]Restore to me the joy of your salvation and grant me a willing spirit, to sustain me. (Psalm 51:1-4; 10-12)

Suggested Prayer

Dear God,

You know the struggles I am having with ongoing sin. Please forgive me my sins. Please deliver me from bondage to sin and create in me a pure heart to live only for you. I rededicate my life to you. Please send your Holy Spirit in all His power to help me live my life exclusively for you. In the name of Jesus, I pray. Amen.

Wisdom & Direction:

[6]Do not be anxious about anything, but in everything, by prayer and petition, with thanksgiving, present your requests to God.[7]And the peace of God, which transcends all understanding, will guard your hearts and your minds in Christ Jesus. (Philippians 4:6-7)

[5]If any of you lacks wisdom, he should ask God, who gives generously to all without finding fault, and it will be given to him. (James 1:5)

Suggested Prayer

Dear God,

You know the situation I face. I don't know what to do. I release my need and my anxieties to you right now and ask that you give me your peace that surpasses understanding, and the wisdom how to resolve my circumstances. Enable me to patiently await your timing for the resolution of the problem and what I need to be doing on my own in the meantime. In the name of Jesus, I pray. Amen.

Physical Healing:

[23]Jesus went throughout Galilee, teaching in their synagogues, preaching the good news of the kingdom, and healing every disease and sickness among the people.[24]News about him spread all over Syria, and people brought to him all who were ill with various diseases, those suffering severe pain, the demon-possessed, those having seizures, and the paralyzed, and he healed them. (Matthew 4:23-24)

Suggested Prayer

Dear God,

I know that you can heal me. You know the pain I am in. I ask that you heal me from my sickness, whether it be divinely or through doctors and medicine. I also know that your will is made perfect through me when I am surrendered to you. If your perfect will does not include my healing, then I ask you to give me the joyful patience of affliction and the peace of heart to glorify you through my illness. In the name of Jesus, I pray. Amen.

Comfort:

[3]Praise be to the God and Father of our Lord Jesus Christ, the Father of compassion and the God of all comfort, [4]who comforts us in all our troubles, so that we can comfort those in any trouble with the comfort we ourselves have received from God.[5]For just as the sufferings of Christ flow over into our lives, so also through Christ our comfort overflows. (2 Corinthians 1:3-5)

Jesus speaking: [28]"Come to me, all you who are weary and burdened, and I will give you rest." (Matthew 11:28)

Suggested Prayer

Dear God,

You know my situation and you know how much I need your comfort in my life right now. Please let me sense your overwhelming love for me right now to see me through the storm I am facing. Please send me your divine comfort and enable me to totally rest in you. In the name of Jesus, I pray. Amen.

Faith & Trust:

[1]Now faith is being sure of what we hope for and certain of what we do not see...

[6]And without faith it is impossible to please God, because anyone who comes to him must believe that he exists and that he rewards those who earnestly seek him. (Hebrews 11:1, 6)

[5]Trust in the Lord with all your heart and lean not on your own understanding; [6]in all your ways acknowledge him, and he will make your paths straight. (Proverbs 3:5-6)

Suggested Prayer

Dear God,

Please give me the faith and trust in you for the circumstance I'm facing. Please develop my faith to think and act in line with your ability to provide, not mine. Please enable me to trust you with all my heart and not to lean on my own understanding. Please teach me to see the incomparably great power you have and not limit myself to my abilities. In the name of Jesus, I pray. Amen.

Protection:

[10]The name of the Lord is a strong tower; the righteous run to it and are safe. (Proverbs 18:10)

Jesus speaking: [33]"I have told you these things, so that in me you may have peace. In this world you will have trouble. But take heart! I have overcome the world." (John 16:33)

Suggested Prayer

Dear God,

You know the life situation I am facing and I am concerned about my safety. I ask for your divine protection. I ask that you send your angels to watch over me and my loved ones. I ask for the peace of heart that Jesus promised in a world filled with trouble. In the name of Jesus, I pray. Amen.

Personal Notes

This section is for you to keep track of your Goals and things you want to or have already achieved. The bible tells us to write the vision and make it plain. If you keep it before you then you will always remember it and therefore continuously be working towards it.

In the first section you can write what area of your life you have a goal for, the steps you will take to obtain it, and then give yourself a deadline so you will keep it in mind. Make sure your goals are reachable but challenging.

In the second section you can write some behaviors, though patterns or habits you wish to change in order to become a better you. Feel free to copy and make more pages.

The last section is for you to list all of your accomplishments along the way. This way you can look back when you reach a rough spot and see where God has taken you and you will have the strength to keep pushing.

Goal Tracking Sheet

I am a princess, daughter of the most High whose praises I will forever sing, the only way to obtain my heart is by humbly going before the King

Proverbs 16:3 Commit to the lord whatever you do and he will establish your plans.

Life Goal	Action Steps	Deadline

Life Goal	Action Steps	Deadline

Goal Tracking Sheet

I am a princess, daughter of the most High whose praises I will forever sing, the only way to obtain my heart is by humbly going before the King

Proverbs 16:3 Commit to the lord whatever you do and he will establish your plans.

Life Goal	Action Steps	Deadline

Life Goal	Action Steps	Deadline

Life Goal	Action Steps	Deadline

Life Goal	Action Steps	Deadline

Checklist

Today is a new Day. I have chosen to change

_____

Things I need to do to change this behavior, thought pattern, or habit

_____
_____
_____
_____
_____
_____
_____
_____

_____
_____
_____
_____
_____
_____

Checklist

Today is a new Day. I have chosen to change

_____

Things I need to do to change this behavior, thought pattern, or habit

_____
_____
_____
_____
_____
_____
_____
_____

_____
_____
_____
_____
_____
_____

Accomplishments

This page is to be used with the goal tracking sheet and checklist to allow you to see what you have been able to accomplish with God's help and Guidance.

_____

_____

_____

_____

_____

_____

_____

Bios

TyJane' Stevens

Leonetta Jules

TyJane' Stevens

TyJane' LeShaun Stevens was born on November 4, 1995 to Leonetta Jules and Brian Hamilton and is also the step-daughter of Maasai Jules. She was born in Hampton Va where she currently resides. She graduated from Phoebus High School class of 2014. She is the oldest of 4 children, her other two sisters are Taneja 13, Precious, 11 and Gabe 3.

She entered a contest and was one of the winners landing her a spot in the Pine Tree Poetry Collection book in 2007. She is also in the 2007/2008 edition of the Who's Who Registry of Academic Excellence and a member of Daughters of Zion DOD since it was founded in 2012. She has a passion for music, ministry, reading and writing. She was stricken with a case of Cerebellar Ataxia at the age of 6, stripping her of the ability to walk and talk and crippled her ability to process and comprehend in most areas. The only thing left intact was her ability to read and write 3 grades above her grade level. It was then that she and her family realized her true purpose. It was with that she began to rebuild, regaining everything she lost and now on a mission to bring God Glory through the gift he gave her, Life and Writing.

Tyjane' was accepted to Chowan University in 2014 as an English major. Currently Tyjane' is pursuing her Associates Degree in Human and Social Services.

Leonetta Jules

Leonetta Rochelle Stevens was born on November 7, 1977 to Mattie and Leonard Stevens. She was born in Hampton VA where she currently resides. She graduated from Phoebus High School with the class of 1996. She had her first child in November of 1995, Tyjane Stevens (who is one of the writers of this book). In November 2007 she married Maasai Jules. They had two more children together, Taneja age 13 and Precious age 11. She is the younger of two children and has one brother Kenneth, a host of nieces, nephews, family & friends.

She studied Criminology at Thomas Nelson Community College, Has a diploma in Paralegal Studies, also a certified Personal Care Aid/CNA, and a Licensed Cosmetologist and owner of New Beginnings Salon.

Her passion for helping teen girls find their purpose in God stemmed from some of her experiences as a young woman, including to succumbing to peer pressure and becoming a teen mother. This book is a result of that passion.

Bibliography

Sunnyside church of the Nazarene: (n.d.) examples of prayer: retrieved 12/01/2012 http://www.sunnysidenazarene.org/pages.asp?pageid=26652

Faith hope love, bible study (n.d.) short prayers-God is Listening: retrieved 12/01/2012 http://www.faith-hope-love-bible-study.com/shortprayers.html

Bible gateway (n.d.) all referenced scriptures: retrieved 12/01/2012 -1/15/2013 http://www.biblegateway.com/

The free dictionary.com (n.d.) all referenced definitions: retrieved 12/01/2012 – 1/ 15/ 2013 http://www.thefreedictionary.com/

Facebook.com (n.d.) all referenced statuses, stories, and poems. : retrieved 12/01/2012- 1/15/2013 referenced as

https://www.facebook.com/tyjane

https://www.facebook.com/arianna.michelle.9

https://www.facebook.com/katrina.pair?fref=ts

Printed in the United States
By Bookmasters